LONDON
CAPITAL CITY

LONDON
CAPITAL CITY

Photographed by Derek Forss
Described by David Pearce

B.T. Batsford Ltd · London

ISBN 0 7134 5362 1

Typeset by Tek-Art Ltd Kent
and printed and bound
in Hong Kong
for the publishers
B.T.Batsford Ltd
4 Fitzhardinge Street
London
W1H 0AH

In respect of the black-and-white illustrations,
acknowledgement is made as follows: British Rail 14
(bottom), 16; Guildhall Library, City of London 49; Royal
Borough of Kensington and Chelsea Public Libraries 18;
London Transport Museum 18; Museum of London 39, 50,
68, 88, 106, 108, 117; Trustees of the Science Museum 14

CONTENTS

THE ILLUSTRATIONS

Colour

Black and White

GLIMPSES

San Francisco? Amsterdam? Istanbul? Kyoto? Venice? London has many surprises and unexpected moods ready to be garnered from a cosmopolitan past and present. Here are (below) Chinese vegetables and the Chinatown gate, Gerrard Street, Soho; the Little Venice area of Paddington, on the old Regent canal; and (opposite, clockwise) the Central London Mosque, Regents Park (designed by Sir Frederick Gibberd); Sir William Chambers's 1761 pagoda in Kew Gardens; a stall in the Portobello Road street market; the Byzantine domes and towers of Westminster Cathedral

Approaches

First there was a primitive settlement in a clearing on the north bank of the river; it was approached on foot and by small boats. Even when the Romans came, two thousand years ago, it was by no means the most important place in southern England. They built a city wall and – most important – a bridge, and made Londinium the capital of their British colony. The city became and remained for nearly two thousand years a significant port, indeed, in the late-nineteenth and early-twentieth centuries, the world's largest.

Until the eighteenth-century development of the stage coach the river was also a main artery for passenger traffic – quicker, safer and more comfortable than riding on muddy, robber-infested roads or tracks. Then came the railway age, with London at the hub of half a dozen national or regional systems – each run by a separate company wanting its own prestigious terminal in the capital. Local railways developed in and around London, in this century all becoming publicly owned. So the transport network evolved: coaches into horse buses into petrol-driven omnibuses; hansom cabs into taxis; surface railways augmented by an underground system to penetrate every part of an already vast metropolis.

These days the foreign visitor will probably arrive by air at one of London's two major airports, and will enter the city by train – surface and/or underground. Possibly, he or she will land at a sea port and drive into town. The Channel Tunnel promises to provide a more direct connection to the Continent.

The City from the Greenwich Observatory

The Royal Observatory (now an astronomy museum), from which this view was taken, has some claim to be the centre of both the navigational and chronological worlds. Here Greenwich Mean Time was established, as well as the prime meridian of longitude. Here we look north-west over Rotherhithe towards the City. The latter, in the light of its importance as a financial centre, is appropriately dominated by Britain's tallest office building, the National Westminster Bank tower

The George Inn at Southwark

Rotherhithe (hithe = a small port) was glimpsed in the preceding view; it is in the north-east corner of the borough of Southwark, which began as a settlement at the south end of the wooden bridge which the Romans built in AD 45. In coaching days, such an inn was the setting-off point for journeys to a coastal port, or, as in the case of Chaucer's pilgrims, to Canterbury. Note the fine wooden balustrades of the 1677 building, which had itself replaced an earlier structure. Now preserved by the National Trust

St Pancras Station

London was the first great city to be served by a railway network radiating nationwide. Great Victorian termini ring the city centre. St Pancras was built of red brick and sandstone by George Gilbert Scott in 1865 for the Midland Railway. There are plans to re-convert this Gothic fantasy of a station forebuilding to its original use as a grand hotel

St Pancras station interior, 1868. The impressive span of Barlow's train shed seen here as it was on completion, with a glimpse of the Midland Railway's 'single wheel' steam locomotives

The ladies' drawing room, first floor, St Pancras hotel, June 1867. A taste of what prospective guests may expect when the proposed re-conversion goes ahead

South Kensington station

A busy local station for a smart inner suburb which became prosperous in Victorian times. London's underground or 'tube' system often rises to the surface, so this view resembles railway stations in many a small English town

The City from Hampstead Heath

From a hill on the side of London directly opposite Greenwich, the City can again be seen. Looking more like farmland, the heath was dense forest in prehistoric times; now it is one of north London's favourite areas for recreation. The lord of the manor sold his rights to the Metropolitan Board of Works in 1871, so the park has been preserved for public use. Other land has been added over the years

CITY ON A RIVER

'Sweet Thames run softly till I end my song'

The origin of the name is unknown; Julius Caesar spoke of the Tamesis. Although London, like most of the world's great cities, grew up on the banks of the river – with trade largely water-borne – its architecture has tended to turn away from the stream. Only the rebuilt Houses of Parliament and Greenwich Hospital, some distance away, have any formal relation with the waterside.

Until the later nineteenth century the river was wide and dirty, being the main receptacle of the city's wastes; muddy banks smelled of refuse and were littered with debris. Much of the south bank was not even built over, apart from Southwark at the south end of London Bridge. The second crossing, at Westminster, was not completed until 1750 and, although the number of bridges rapidly increased, the south side remained comparatively insignificant. Most of the population was crammed into the walled city and yet, even when that 'great wen' was at its peak of noise, dirt, smoke and squalor, the Thames was a symbol of spaciousness. Several times in the sixteenth and seventeenth centuries, when it froze over, the river was the setting for huge fairs; oxen were roasted on the thick ice.

Teeming with shipping for centuries, the Thames – which is now cleaner and well embanked, with good access along much of its waterfront – is comparatively uncrowded. The port has moved downstream, labour resistance to new technology having hastened London Pool's decline. Tourist boats ply for custom, but there is no regular river bus service.

An eighteenth-century view of Westminster Bridge, from Lambeth. Westminster Abbey (left) would be invisible from this position today, concealed behind the then unbuilt Houses of Parliament

Canaletto's *View Up River to Westminster. Westminster Abbey is visible here to the right of the half-completed Westminster Bridge. The 'shot tower' on the right was used for testing ammunition*

The Thames from Hungerford Bridge

*Nineteenth-century embankments reduced the width of the water course to about half its natural
extent. On the south bank (right) can be seen the concrete terraces and fly towers of the National
Theatre, designed by Denys Lasdun in the early 1970s. Waterloo Bridge was last rebuilt in 1937-42*

The City from Waterloo Bridge

The north bank view shows the Savoy hotel on the left, St Paul's Cathedral with its eloquent dome behind the two west towers in the centre, and the skyscrapers of the financial district on the right. The embankment gardens were created when the river width was reduced here in 1870. Vessels moored beside it are mostly pleasure steamers for tourists to see London's sights from the water

The Thames Embankment. Its construction was undertaken from 1864-70: the new thoroughfare speeded up the flow of traffic, but distanced many buildings from the waterfront. St Pauls dominates the City's skyline. The Monument can be seen above the third arch of Blackfriars Bridge, commemorating the Great Fire of 1666. An interesting comparison with the same view today (opposite)

Part of London Bridge, by John Varley. Peter of Colechurch began construction of the bridge in 1176: it took 35 years to complete, but was in use for over 600. The bridge was finally replaced in 1834, but the nineteenth-century structure has since been transported stone-by-stone to Lake Havasu in Arizona. The present structure was completed in 1972

The Thames at sunset from Tower Bridge

Even warehouses and industrial buildings look romantic in such a light. No wonder riverside conversions of such disused buildings are being undertaken in great numbers and are selling for high prices

Battersea power station

Battersea was a Thames-side village about three miles from London, with market gardening as its main industry, until the late-nineteenth century. Now the area boasts a large riverside park, a populous residential area to the south and a large power station. This was started by the architect Sir Giles Gilbert Scott in the late 1930s, completed in the early '50s, closed in the '70s, and preserved for proposed leisure uses in the '80s

Tower Bridge

One of London's most famous sights, this is yet another achievement of Victorian engineering. The only bridge down-river from London Bridge, is was built with a 'bascule' in the 1890s; thus two vast spans can be raised, as if on hinges, to provide a clear opening 200 feet wide, with a headroom of 135 feet. The structure was designed in the Gothic style, quite unlike the 'Child with a Dolphin' fountain in the foreground. This last is a feature of recent embankment improvements

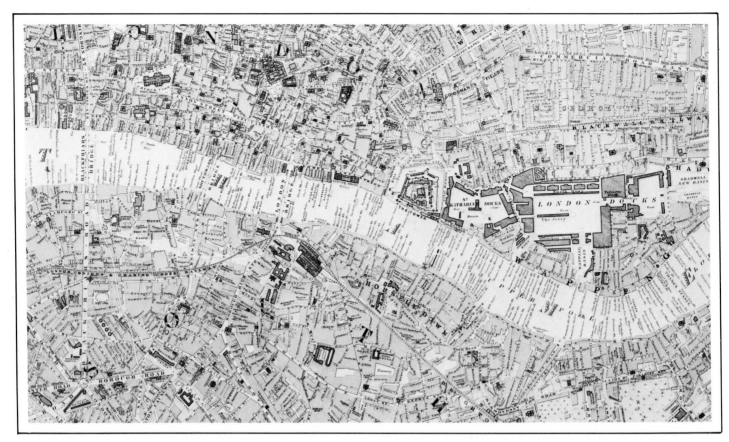

The City and docks, from Stanford's Library Map of London and its Suburbs, c. 1863. St Katherine's Dock is clearly visible, as well as the Tower of London and St Paul's Cathedral. Tower Bridge isn't marked: it wasn't constructed until the 1890s. The old docklands area is now the focus for intense urban development – redrawing the map once again

St Katherine's dock

The first of the great nineteenth-century docks was built in the 1820s on some 20 acres just east of the north end of Tower Bridge. Its basin is now a yacht haven and the former warehouses accommodate variously housing, offices, shops and restaurants. Sadly, several of the buildings have been largely rebuilt, but the collection of historic vessels is, in the main part, genuine

The Cutty Sark

This preserved sailing ship on King William Walk at Greenwich is the last and most famous of the tea clippers. Built at Dumbarton in 1869, she has been permanently berthed in a dry dock since 1954. Inside is a collection of maritime relics, pictures and figureheads

Blackfriars Bridge

Most Thames bridges are for road traffic but here two crossings were built in the 1860s and 1880s for the London, Chatham and Dover Railway. The red-painted, Romanesque-style cast iron columns of the western bridge can be seen in the foreground, with Brunel's later arches beyond

The Tower of London from Tower Bridge

Ancient and modern towers. William the Conqueror's great Norman fortress was one of several built to subdue the vanquished Saxons. It was also a royal palace as well as a grim prison, but now has a happier role as a major historic tourist attraction. Some three million visitors are shown round each year by the Beefeaters (warders), dressed as they were in the reign of Henry VIII. To the left can be seen the City financial district again

Greenwich Tunnel entrance

Besides a dozen or so bridges, there are a few tunnels dug through the Thames clay. This one connects Greenwich and the 'Isle of Dogs', a docklands area to the north. It was built in the 1900s as a route for dock workers. The length is over 1200 feet. Photographed here on an Autumn evening is the north shaft, with a domed glass roof for stairs and lifts

ARCHITECTURAL HERITAGE

A centre of wealth, power and culture for a thousand years, London has – despite fires, bombs and developers – preserved a heritage of architecture unique in its scope and variety. This is partly because London 'just grew'; its vested interests successfully resisting any attempts to replan extensive parts of the city on formal lines. Charm resides in the small scale, sometimes higgledy-piggledy character of a place often said to consist of an amalgam of villages. Even the great buildings tend to arrest the attention of the onlooker more by their rich detail than their breathtaking grandeur.

St Paul's Cathedral was always an exception to the small scale of the capital; Old St Paul's was one of the outstanding churches in Christendom, with a spire 450 feet high. Itself a successor to several churches on the site since AD 604 , it was destroyed with most of the rest of the City in the Great Fire of 1666. Another more modest cathedral across the river at Southwark started life as a priory. Westminster was an abbey, only a little more prominent than several others in or near London such as those at Bermondsey and Waltham; it became England's most famous church because many monarchs are buried at Westminster and almost all were crowned there. There were hundreds of parish churches before the Fire and scores afterwards. Of the several London castles, only the Norman Tower of London survives. Spencer House stands as one of the few surviving examples of the great town houses of the nobility – Apsley House is another. These private palaces once dominated the capital, alongside the churches their owners helped to build. They lined the banks of the Thames and were later the *raison d'être* of Piccadilly, St James's Square and Park Lane. Their richness can be guessed from the surviving handful and from such royal residences as St James's Palace, Hampton Court, Kew and Kensington palaces. Many of Sir Christopher Wren's post-fire churches were restored after World War II.

Extensive urban improvements were carried out, for the Prince Regent – at the beginning of the nineteenth century – by architect John Nash. Painted stucco palace-style fronts lined Regents Park, Portland Place, Regent Street and the Mall to Buckingham Palace itself.

Developments in this century have been, by international standards, small scale – for much the same reasons as in the past. Despite much unnecessary demolition, London remains a gracious town of brick, stucco and stone – with concrete, steel and glass only dominant in enclaves such as the South Bank Arts Centre and the City.

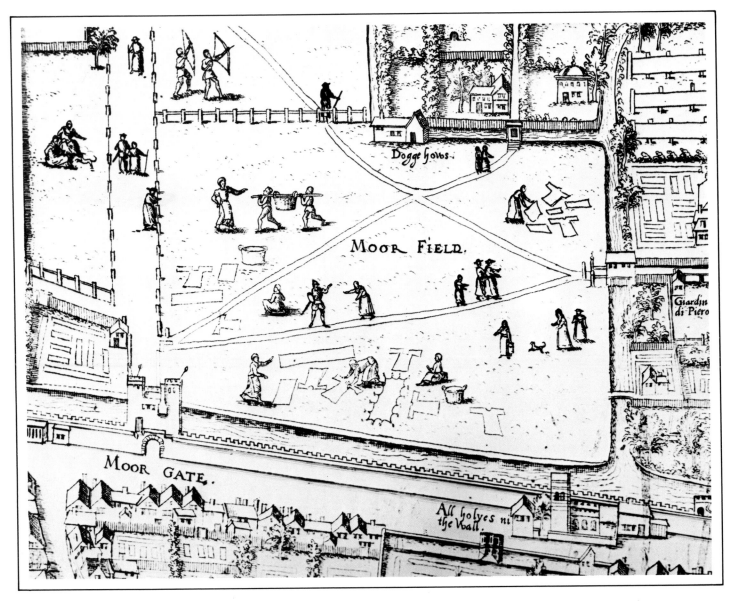

Doggе hовѕ.

MOOR FIELD.

Giardin di Piero

MOOR GATE.

All holyes ni the Woall

Fleet Street and St Paul's Cathedral

Named after the former river Fleet, a Thames tributary, this thoroughfare has long been synonymous with the national press in Britain. Until recently it was lined with the headquarters of newspapers selling many millions daily, but, in a few years, almost all of them will have moved to new homes in the former Docklands. The railway bridge is on the site of the former Ludgate, an entrance through the city walls into the 'square mile' of the original London. Post-war office blocks and a Wren parish church steeple preface the north-west tower and 365 foot dome of the architect's masterpiece

Moorfield, from a Map of London engraved in 1558-9. Moorgate survives as a name: this area is now the site of the Barbican arts and residential complex

St John's Gate, Clerkenwell

Built in 1504, this was one of the main entrances to the priory of St John of Jerusalem. After the dissolution of the monasteries it was converted to a succession of uses. In 1877 the St John's Ambulance Brigade was founded here. The building now contains a museum. Though much restored, it is a reminder of the city's many medieval gates, long since destroyed but commemorated in such names as Aldgate and Newgate

Royal Naval College, Greenwich

This impressive riverside complex in Portland stone was started as a royal palace for Charles II in 1669. Funds ran out, and the buildings were eventually completed to designs by Wren and Hawksmoor in a splendidly confident classical style at the end of the century. Never fitted out as the intended palace, it was at first a naval hospital, then a naval college, now one for the combined services

BRASS GUN (SIAMESE)

THIS BRASS GUN, MADE ABOUT 1623
AT SINGORA IN SIAM AND CAPTURED
BY THE BURMANS AT AYUTHIA IN 1767,
WAS TAKEN BY THE BRITISH IN THE
THIRD BURMESE WAR 1885 - 1887.
THE GUN BEARS INSCRIPTIONS IN
ARABIC, MALAY AND BURMESE ONE
OF WHICH REFERS TO SULAYMAN
SHAH THE VICTORIOUS KING.

Royal Hospital, Chelsea

Yet another creation of Sir Christopher Wren, this home for retired soldiers is in the more domestically scaled red brick and stone-dressed classicism of most eighteenth-century manor houses. The 'Chelsea Pensioners' still enliven the local scene with their bright red uniform coats

Hampton Court Palace

The great gatehouse of a residence built by Henry VIII's chancellor, Cardinal Wolsey, and donated by that subject to his monarch in a vain attempt to retain royal support. The original entrance of 1515 is a good example of early Tudor brickwork. The gable end of the great hall added by the king himself is on the left

Tudor Pond Garden, Hampton Court

Seven miles upstream from Westminster, on the north bank of the Thames, Hampton Court became a country retreat for the monarchy. Its majestic gardens and avenues of lime trees are now an oasis of green in suburbia. Henry VIII's grounds originally included herb gardens, bowers, shady walks, and the renowned Mount Garden surmounted by an array of heraldic beasts. All that now remains is the Pond Garden, restored in 1924

Guildhall, City of London

This building has also suffered devastating damage, in particular in the Great Fire of London in 1666 and in World War II bombing. The entrance façade of the London 'town hall', and indeed of the hall within, were originally of the fifteenth century, heavily restored in the seventeenth and nineteenth centuries and reinstated again in the 1950s. The canopy on the left is part of the west wing, containing offices and the Guildhall Library, which was added in 1974

Spencer House, Green Park

One of the few surviving private palaces of the British aristocracy. This Palladian mansion of the 1740s is still owned by the Spencer family – the 21st birthday ball of Princess Diana's brother took place there recently. However the building is normally rented and has not been been occupied as the family home for over two generations

A FINANCIAL HUB

The 'richest square mile in the world' was the City's pre-World War II boast – the capital 'C' having long denoted the financial quarter which roughly coincided with the old walled city and, indeed, the city of the Romans. Even in late medieval times, London was a wealthy city. The outstanding Lord Mayor Sir Richard ('Dick') Whittington – who came in fact from a relatively well-to-do background – left a fortune at his death in 1423 'equivalent to the wealth of a medium-sized kingdom'.

The legend of streets 'paved with gold' referred to a city which was externally much less impressive to look at than that of today's expanding banking, commodity, stock-broking and insurance markets. But even the present sky-scrapered City has proved unable to supply large open-plan offices quickly enough to match the demand. Vast office developments are projected in the old Docklands area, east of the Tower of London.

The Royal Exchange, 1897. Late-nineteenth-century commentators worried about the congestion of traffic en route *from the City to the West End!*

Victorian Cheapside, with the tower of St Mary le Bow on the left and the dome of St Paul's looming behind

The City from the Monument

The mercantile, banking and broking functions of the City of London, established when it was the heart of the world's greatest trading empire, have survived longer than other aspects of global power. Insurance, money and commodity markets continue to thrive, because of entrepreneurial skills, because English is the dominant language of commerce and because of London's convenient position in terms of clock-time between New York and Tokyo. Much of the City was flattened during the War. Immediate post-War buildings in the foreground contrast with taller and later glass towers behind

The Royal Exchange and Bank

The core of the City still has an appearance of solid, old-world masonry. The Bank of England on the left was largely rebuilt in the 1920s. The Royal Exchange, with its giant portico, has long ago lost its role as a meeting place for merchants. Behind the Bank rises the 1960s Stock Exchange and behind that the National Westminster Bank tower

Reuter statue

A recently installed commemorative bust beside the Royal Exchange building. 'Reuters' operates today in nearly every country; the company has greatly expanded as the provider of worldwide, electronically transmitted financial information as well as the long established general news services

Lloyd's Building from the Monument

An insurance headquarters viewed from the top of the column commemorating one of the most expensive disasters ever; the Great Fire of London in 1666. The new Lloyd's is the latest in a series of buildings to house the world's premier insurance market, which originated in Edward Lloyd's coffee house in the 1680s. This edifice, opened by the Queen in 1986, is the work of architect Richard Rogers

SEAT OF GOVERNMENT

The country was governed from wherever the king had his Court, sometimes not in London at all, but generally first in the City, then Westminster, Whitehall, St James's and finally Buckingham Palace. By the time the last was royally occupied, in the later eighteenth century, government was overwhelmingly a function of parliament and therefore centred on Westminster and Whitehall. In the next century, palatial ministerial offices were added to the few earlier ones, such as the Admiralty. The Foreign, Home, War and Scottish offices as well as the Treasury lined Whitehall.

Buckingham Palace, a major formal gesture and place of ceremony, has never been particularly popular among monarchs as a place to live. The great parades which terminate here pass and ignore the real seat of power, a modest looking Georgian brick terrace called Downing Street. But Sir Charles Barry and Augustus Pugin ensured that Parliament itself was housed in a building of distinction, after the old building was burned down in 1834.

Considering Britain's military might over many centuries – or perhaps because of the assurance that came from always fighting wars on other people's land – the presence of armed forces in the capital is, like that of the sovereign, largely historic and ceremonial. Foot and Horse Guards in centuries-old uniform styles watch over Buckingham and St James's palaces, Clarence House, the home of the Queen Mother, and their own headquarters at Horse Guards Parade, Whitehall.

White Tower, Tower of London

The keep was the central stronghold in all early medieval castles. On the eastern edge of a city of small wooden houses, this one must have been an awesome sight. It remained a royal palace and administrative headquarters until early Tudor times

Whitehall and Earl Haig's statue

Elizabeth I extended, albeit haphazardly, her father's palace of Whitehall. In early Stuart times there were over 2000 rooms occupied by the Court. Burnt down in 1698, the name survives as the street of government buildings. The statue of the most famous First World War general is on the left. Trafalgar Square beyond is dominated by the monument to the far more brilliant Admiral Nelson. The dome and portico constitute the central features of the National Gallery

Parliament Square and Westminster Abbey

At the further end of Whitehall is the 'west minster'; that is, a monastery to the west of London – one of England's chief ecclesiastical centres for a thousand years. Alongside the church was yet another royal palace (it still technically is one) in which Parliament sat. The square in its present form is a post-War creation

Westminster Bridge and Big Ben

After another major fire had destroyed the old palace of Westminster in 1834, Charles Barry won the architectural competition to rebuild Parliament 'in the Gothic or Elizabethan style'. His building partakes of both and yet is like nothing before conceived. The Czar of Russia called it 'a dream in stone'. This uniqueness, especially of the clock tower with its famous chime, has secured his building worldwide familiarity as an image of London and, indeed, Britain

Burghers of Calais Memorial, Victoria Tower Gardens

The civic leaders of Calais offered themselves, with ropes around their necks, to persuade the victorious English King Edward III to spare their town in 1347. Rodin's group was installed in the Calais Place Richelieu in 1895. This cast was positioned in the shadow of the Victoria Tower at the west end of the Houses of Parliament in 1915

Horse Guards in the Mall

Another image of military and state pageantry for which London is renowned. These soldiers represent some of the oldest regiments of the British army and still carry out their role – now largely ceremonial – of protecting the monarch. When not posted in London, however, they can be found on duty equipped as modern servicemen

Admiralty Arch

Only in the early years of this century was a processional way created to link the royal palace with Trafalgar Square and on to Westminster, for such occasions as the state opening of Parliament. Admiralty Arch faces Buckingham Palace along the length of the Mall

Stable Yard, St James's

Another of Henry VIII's building ventures was the enlargement of the leper hospital of St James into another palace. Some of his buildings survive, though here the footguards in their bearskins are patrolling beside the Georgian additions. On the right is the former ducal mansion, Lancaster House, now used for government conferences and entertaining

Buckingham Palace

Here is the view across the lake in St James's Park which, like most of central London's open spaces, was at one time a royal pleasure ground. The present palace was the Duke of Buckingham's house, originally situated in a pleasant, semi-rural setting. Bought by George III in 1762, rebuilt by George IV, enlarged by Queen Victoria – whose gilded monument can be seen on the right – the palace was finally refronted in Portland stone in 1913

Buckingham Palace – a Georgian view. Much the same vista can be enjoyed today by strollers in St James's Park

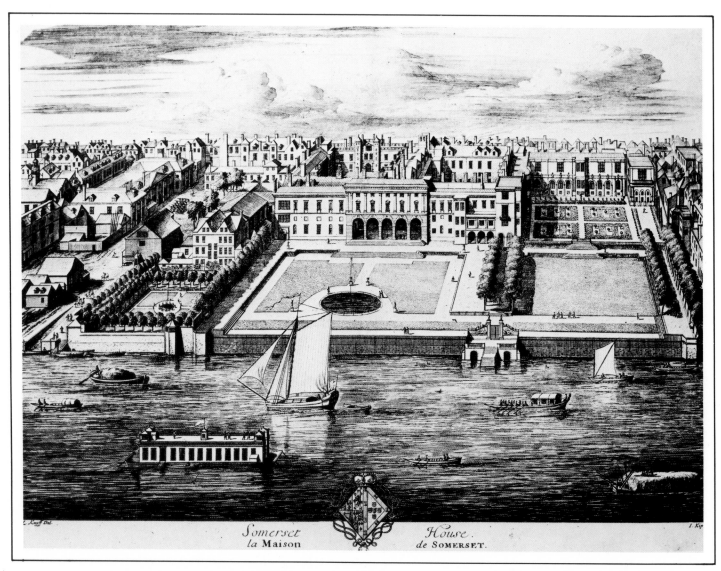

Somerset *House.*
la Maison *de* SOMERSET.

By the sixteenth century, the waterfront between Westminster and Temple was lined with the mansions of the nobility. One of the first to be built was the original Somerset House for the Duke of Somerset in 1547. The later Somerset House, Britain's oldest Government office, now occupies this site

Somerset House and the Embankment

The site of an aristocratic riverside mansion, this was rebuilt by architect William Chambers from about 1775 – the first purpose-built government offices. Now the fine interiors are being refurbished to contain overflows from the national art collections. Before the Thames embankments were built, the river lapped against the arches of the south terrace, visible on the lower right

CITY OF TEMPLES

London is not the seat of the Primate of All England, a distinction which belongs to Canterbury. It is, however, the place that English Catholics look to, in the person of the Cardinal Archbishop of Westminster. Westminster Cathedral, Britain's most important Catholic church, is a colourful exuberance of Byzantine-inspired Victorian brickwork. A great capital has many central functions; medicine, learning and the law all tend to have their leading exponents there. There are several universities and many colleges containing tens of thousands of students; London's teaching hospitals are outstanding, and the law courts and the 'Inns' where lawyers have their chambers (and where a few still live) are all in London. There are interesting buildings occupied by academics, doctors and lawyers, but they do not dominate the city, for they all derive from antecedent institutions, the monarchy and the church.

All the old European cities expressed in their fabric the pre-eminence of religion. This life being but an uncomfortable passage to the next, the buildings which towered over the temporal city would naturally be those most closely related to the journey. The resources and energies of thousands of people – and London was a metropolis of about 50,000 in the fourteenth century – were directed to the construction and adornment of one great edifice, the cathedral. Its closest rivals in scale were other churches, those of important and rich monastic orders. The skyline of the pre-Great Fire city and, indeed, the eighteenth-century one, was dominated by St Paul's Cathedral, Westminster Abbey and the towers of dozens of major churches and many smaller ones.

Now there is religious plurality at a time when the traditional churches have ceased to play such a vital role in most lives. Besides the Catholic cathedral there is a Greek Orthodox one near Oxford Street. There are Methodist and other Non Conformist chapels and meeting houses, Polish churches, synagogues and mosques. In this sphere, as in several others, London's variety seems almost infinite.

Lambeth Palace

On the south bank of the river, Lambeth Palace remains the London home of the Primate of All England, the Archbishop of Canterbury; the senior cleric of the Anglican communion throughout the world. This gatehouse is one of London's few surviving medieval buildings. The Victoria tower can be seen across the river

Westminster Abbey

The east end of one of England's oldest and most historic churches is entirely French in character. The abbey, originally built in the seventh century on what was an island in the marshes west of London, became a national church under Edward the Confessor in 1040. This view over the high altar shows the choir built in about 1260, in the lofty apsidal form of the cathedrals of the Isle de France. Many British monarchs have been married and buried here and almost all were crowned at Westminster

Henry VII's chapel, Westminster Abbey

Continuing beyond the choir, this chapel was started by Henry VII in 1503. Buried there in 1509, he was followed by other Tudor monarchs. This building is one of the greatest examples of Gothic Perpendicular, developed in England when much of the rest of Europe had adopted Renaissance architectural forms.

St Bartholomew's, Smithfield

*A great Norman church, London's oldest, this is the only surviving part of an Augustinian priory
founded in 1123. Much restored, it remains both movingly austere and venerable*

St Clement Danes

Wren built more than 50 parish churches to replace the many destroyed in the Great Fire. He achieved the maximum effect on crowded and restricted sites by designing intricate and lofty spires. Essentially Gothic in character, they were almost all completed in his personal version of Renaissance style. 'The bells of St Clement's are remembered in the child's nursery rhyme, 'Oranges and Lemons'

St Martin in the Fields

During the years 1722-4, the architect James Gibbs adapted Wren's formula to create a church design with a high steeple, curiously – and successfully – perched on a Roman temple-style portico. This form was followed widely for over a century, especially in North America. In the foreground is one of Trafalgar Square's fountains, and on the left the eastern end of the National Gallery

St Paul's Cathedral, 1743. Such an unimpeded view of Wren's masterpiece is now impossible: multi-storey development of the City has hemmed it in on every side

St Paul's Cathedral

This view, looking east towards the high altar, gives some impression of the scale of Wren's masterpiece, which took over half a century to construct. The choir was hit by a bomb in the last war and the elaborate baroque baldacchino over the altar was a post-War design, replacing a less successful Victorian reredos

The dome of St Paul's

The chief glory of the cathedral. The vast mural by Sir James Thornhill, with its architectural trompe l'œil, *magnifies the effect of grandeur. In the centre is the opening towards the cupola which, topped by its gold cross, rises above the surrounding city*

St Paul's: the crypt

While most national heroes are buried and commemorated in Westminster Abbey, some of the most outstanding lie in this impressive undercroft beneath the floor of St Paul's. On Wren's own tablet is found the inscription 'si monumentum requiris, circumspice'. But even more moving is Nelson's black and gold tomb seen here

PARKS AND GARDENS

The English have always had a sentimental attraction to nature. Unbuilt land dedicated to recreation does not occur in a city in any automatic way. There was no significant park in either of the old cities of London or Westminster. Until the nineteenth century the built-up area was small enough to allow access to nearby country. The essential 'lungs' of the later metropolis have been created largely by means of the gift by the sovereign of what had been gardens and grounds of various palaces and residences – on the urban fringe until engulfed by the sprawl.

So Hyde Park was a royal manor and deer park, having once been an ecclesiastical one. St James's Park had also been attached to a royal property, having been detached from a church one. Kensington Gardens had been the pleasure ground of that palace. Regent's Park had also been Crown land. So all of London's chief places of open-air recreation remain 'royal parks', with the large and notable exception of Hampstead Heath. This was sold by the lord of the manor to the Metropolitan Board of Works in 1871, and has been extended since by the the kind of municipal enterprise responsible for creating other large tracts of recreational land further into the suburbs.

Hogarth's Green Park, 1760. Spencer House can be seen at the centre left: Westminster Abbey in the distance. The park at this time stood at the western extremity of the capital

Kenwood House

On the edge of Hampstead Heath, this is essentially a
brick-built manor house of about 1700 which was
remodelled by the great neo-classical architect Robert
Adam, some 60 years later. A property of the earls of
Mansfield for nearly two centuries, the estate was vested in
the London County Council in 1924 and opened to the
public a year later. In 1927 Lord Iveagh – owner of the
house, its splended picture collection and immediate
grounds – bequeathed them to the nation. Open air
concerts are held here in summer

Hyde Park Corner and Apsley House

The mansion was long known as 'No 1, London', being at the north-western extremity of development. Beyond was open land as far as the village of Knightsbridge. The house was re-built and enlarged by the Duke of Wellington, after the battle of Waterloo and his return from several years as arbiter of the peace of Europe. A monument to the 'Iron Duke' can be seen in the foreground. Apsley House (he kept the earlier name) contains a splendid collection of paintings as well as military trophies. The Duke's descendants still have an apartment here

The Grand Entrance to Hyde Park, 1846; Decimus Burton's Screen, built 1810, still graces Hyde Park Corner

Kensington Gardens

Almost an extension of Hyde Park, Kensington Gardens are, typically of London, a mixture – of formal gardens, walks and ponds, as well as 'natural landscape'. They were first laid out as part of the grounds of Kensington Palace

Albert Memorial

The immense, multi-coloured Albert Memorial was erected by Queen Victoria in memory of her beloved consort. Designed by Sir George Gilbert Scott and erected in 1863-72, it was for decades ridiculed as an extreme example of Victorian taste, then unfashionable; but its elaborate ornament has come to be admired

Model boats sailing on the round pond in Kensington Gardens c. 1910

TEMPLE OF VICTORY

HERMITAGE

RUINED ARCH

CHINESE PAGODA, KEW GARDENS

CHINESE TEMPLE

The architect Sir William Chambers designed several follies for the Royal Botanic Gardens at Kew, most famous of which is the pagoda (page 9)

Kensington Gardens: the Peter Pan statue

A contrast with the grandiloquent Victorian Gothic pile is this playful reminder of an imaginary character who stands for another aspect of Victorian and Edwardian sentimentality. James Barry's play Peter Pan *is still regularly performed each Christmas. The statue itself dates from 1912*

Regents Park; Queen Mary's Gardens

Here two kinds of artefact are pointedly set against carefully contrived nature. It is a bold artist who casts a metal bird for a setting often enlivened by the real thing. Beyond the park emerges the 620 feet high Post Office Tower. This communications centre – recently renamed by its owner, British Telecom – was completed in 1964. Unfortunately, the revolving restaurant and viewing platform are now closed to the public

Fitzroy Square

Another kind of public garden has been created in Robert Adam's splendid late eighteenth-century square. Perhaps the present informal layout mismatches a little with the continuous 'palace façade' surrounding it – but a bronze by the late Henry Moore is a welcome addition

St Luke's Gardens, Chelsea

Many of London's smaller parks can show similarly spectacular combinations of exotic and indigenous trees, flowers and shrubs

ENTERTAINMENTS

A capital city is also a place to have fun. Theatres, cinemas, hotels, shops, museums, street markets and pubs provide focuses for leisure. The marketing and distribution of food and other essentials have always been a crucial city function; now even shopping for pleasure cannot be regarded as entirely frivolous, since tourism rivals commerce and finance as a source of national income.

London's museums, like its theatres largely nineteenth-century in origin and appearance, are incomparable. The collections of the British Museum, the National Gallery and the Victoria and Albert Museum can scarcely be rivalled in quality, and certainly not in quantity, elsewhere. But these are only the 'flagships'; dozens of other major collections and shows are there to be explored and experienced, mostly without the inconvenience of being charged for admission.

The theatres, both subsidized and commercial, such as the National and Royal Shakespeare on the one hand and most of the West End and the ever-growing 'fringe' on the other, are also excellent by international standards. London has more permanent symphony orchestras than any other city; it also has two major opera and ballet houses, Covent Garden and the Coliseum.

Of course there is also pop music, in which London plays a leading world role. Recording studios, discos and jazz clubs abound. And as for shopping, it only need be said that the English are still happy to be referred to as a nation of shop-keepers – the label first given by Napoleon as an intended insult.

Christmas lights in Regent Street

The annual decorations in the West End are designed to a series of co-ordinated themes each year and financed by local traders. Many tourists are attracted by the lights, which blend well with the neon advertisements

Queen Elizabeth Hall, the Hayward Gallery, Royal Festival Hall and the Shell Centre

The South Bank arts centre was a major municipal enterprise, undertaken after the 1951 Festival of Britain on the site. The embankment was improved and concrete and stone buildings now dominate this stretch of the river. Now there is a scheme to humanize this weatherstained complex. In contrasting style, the 1962 Shell Building represents the attempt to combine commercial monumentality and skyscraper scale

*Piccadilly Circus, 1900. Victorian traffic circulates under
the Eros statue. Surviving buildings include the London
Pavilion on the left, and the Criterion Theatre (page 110)
on the right*

The Eros statue in
Piccadilly Circus

*This awkward confluence of West End streets has never
worked architecturally or as a traffic island, yet its position
at the heart of theatreland has made it renowned. Alfred
Gilbert's perhaps unintentionally jolly memorial to the
philanthropic seventh earl of Shaftesbury was intended to
represent the angel of Christian charity rather than the God
of Love. The first London statue cast in aluminium, it was
unveiled in 1893 and restored at great expense in 1986*

The British Museum

A view under the massive stone portico of Smirke's neo-classical entrance façade demonstrates the lasting beauty of masonry. The museum's collection was based on that of the physician, Sir Hans Sloane, which passed to the nation at his death in 1753. It has been augmented by purchases and gifts ranging from royal libraries to items brought by Captain Cook from the South Seas, Egyptian antiquities, the Elgin marbles, David Garrick's old plays and antiquities from every corner of the globe

Sunday painters' show on Piccadilly

Another form of decoration is provided free on the railings of Green Park on Sundays. An opportunity to browse and even buy a fairly inexpensive memento of a visit

Regency London was noted for the elegance of its fashions. The Burlington Arcade was occupied on its opening in 1819 by hosiers, glovers, milliners and the like

Burlington Arcade

High quality, high style and high priced merchandise are found in the speciality shops in Covent Garden and in covered shopping arcades such as this. Built beside the former mansion of the earls of Burlington (now the Royal Academy) when the family needed to raise funds, this is a miniature version of a design more common in continental Europe

Covent Garden

Originally the grounds of a convent, then a seventeenth-century piazza intended for aristocratic residences, this was for two centuries London's premier fruit and vegetable market. Threatened with demolition during the 1960s' municipal redevelopment mania, it was just preserved by an official change of policy. Now the well restored and paved quarter – with its boutiques, restaurants, bars and outdoor entertainers – has upstaged Carnaby Street and the King's Road as a favoured outdoor rendezvous

The Piazza at Covent Garden. Laid out in the 1630s, it was London's first residential square. This view shows Inigo Jones's church of St Paul's at the west overlooking the central space later filled by the market

The Criterion Theatre

'The stillness of the theatre, before or after the performance'. No visit to London would be complete without a sampling of the capital's theatreland, whether your tastes run to Shakespeare or Andrew Lloyd Webber

The TV-AM building at Camden Lock

The late-eighteenth and early-nineteenth centuries saw a sizeable canal system skirting London, especially on the north side. Typical of the post 1970s re-use of former warehouse and industrial buildings is this highly successful and entertaining conversion to studios by architect Terry Farrell. As befits a base for breakfast TV, the many-gabled building is crowned with egg cups!

Portobello Road market

A contrast to the Chinese markets in Gerrard Street, many of the vegetables here are associated with the cuisine of the Caribbean. Originally a track to a farm, called 'Porto Bello' after a naval victory of 1739, a street market was established here in 1870. On the edge of town, a mile or so west of Hyde Park, it was once used by horse dealers. Antiques now predominate at the south end near Notting Hill, graduating to second-hand clothes, junk shops and food at the north. The crowds come on Saturdays — but the real bargain hunter needs to arrive very early in the morning!

The Kings Road, Chelsea

*Punks have become another universal London symbol, but
the Kings Road is a promenade for anyone who wants to be
seen. It's here that designers go to copy new fashions
'off the street'*

South Molton Street

*The area near Bond Street is geared for the shopper attuned
to the most exclusive fashions. In the surrounding streets
can be found the London outlets of the top British,
Continental, Japanese and American designers*

A PLACE TO LIVE

Unless you are one of the several million municipal tenants, it is expensive to live in London – and even these 'council' properties are likely to cost more to rent here than elsewhere. Much of the population has moved out to the suburbs or leapt over the 'green belt' imposed in 1940s to contain the urban sprawl – and so have created a city-region of over 20 million people. The gracious eighteenth and nineteenth-century squares, streets, and mews are occupied by either the rich or those too poor to migrate to the suburbs. The latter used to live as servants in the basements and over the stables (or mews); now even these are owned by the well-to-do. Inner-city boroughs such as Westminster, Kensington and Chelsea, Islington and Camden are all inhabited by such a disparate mix.

The process of improvement and conversion (often labelled 'gentrification') has resulted in many areas being better kept and more thoughtfully decorated than ever before. The quality of gardens, both private and public, is impressive. Until recently Londoners lived on the ground – in houses, not apartments. Even near the centre the tall, narrow terraced house was the norm. Victorian and Edwardian 'mansion blocks' of flats did change the pattern slightly, but to a much smaller extent than in most European cities. Occasionally of stone, often plastered and painted, or just handsome brickwork alone, the London house was essentially a Georgian creation. Today this type is valued more than ever.

Corner shops and local centres, an extensive bus and underground railway system and pleasant safe streets through which to walk have meant that London has not surrendered to the motor car as completely as many big towns. The human scale implied in the phrase 'a city of villages' persists, despite the fact that road traffic is usually present. The many parks and gardens, the tree-lined streets and squares, combine to make it in many parts a green and pleasant place.

Park Village East, by Thomas Shepherd, 1829. This was one of the two groups of villas planned by John Nash to the east of Regents Park

Chester Terrace, Regents Park

One of John Nash's splendid neo-classical terraces built for the Prince Regent, this is a beautiful combination of nature and architecture north of London's bustling West End. Still part of the Crown Estate, these houses are partly occupied by institutions, partly still residential

Pelham Crescent

A little later and a good deal more modest, but still in the same plaster on brick neo-classical vein, this terrace is typical of small-scale nineteenth-century residential London. Now a quiet and desirable neighbourhood in South Kensington

Pelham Place

Nearby is this still more modestly developed residential area with cottage-like houses. This is also now quite an affluent neighbourhood, as the well maintained gardens suggest

Kensington Park Estate, Notting Hill, looking east; T. Allom, 1853. During the 1850s and 60s a fashionable new residential area emerged on the slopes to the north of Notting Hill Gate. The spacious plan combined terraces and semi-detached villas in sweeping curves, enclosing large communal gardens

Kensington Palace Gardens

Later and more pretentious than the Pelham estate, these big houses near Kensington Palace are now largely occupied by embassies. The robust Victorian mail box reminds us of another British contribution to civilization – the stamped letter post

Folgate Street, Spitalfields

An early eighteenth-century house in the Huguenot weavers quarter, east of the City; this has been imaginatively restored as a living museum in a newly revived area. Once the monastic Hospital of St Mary occupied much of the area

Colville Place

These late-eighteenth-century artisans' dwellings were in a narrow street (now a pedestrian precinct) just north of the colour and bustle of Oxford Street. In poor condition, scheduled for demolition in the 1960s and for preservation in the 1970s (such are the vagaries of local government), the houses have been restored as an expensive residential enclave in an area of offices and restaurants

Shepherd Market

Edward Shepherd was a builder and developer operating on and to the south of the fabulously wealthy Grosvenor Estate in the early-eighteenth century. This small and intricate group of narrow streets was, until recently, a locale of 'houses of ill repute'. Now it is an area for galleries, small shops and restaurants, as well as pieds-à-terre for the fortunate few

Admiral's Walk, Hampstead

Here one can readily see how the rural charms of Hampstead village, with its hills and fresh air a few miles north-west of the grim and smoky City, attracted many nineteenth-century residents. Among them were John Keats and Charles Dickens

Strand on the Green

This is a pre-Georgian suburb fronting the Thames in Chiswick. William Hogarth lived nearby, and is buried in Chiswick churchyard

Royal Avenue, Chelsea

Away from the bustle of the Kings Road, Chelsea remains an elegant residential district. The terraced late-Georgian architecture is typical of so many of London's most attractive neighbourhoods